taylor lautner

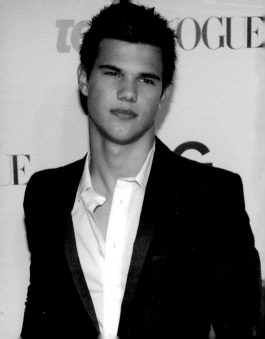

taylor
lautner

SARAH PARVIS

Andrews McMeel
Publishing, LLC

Kansas City • Sydney • London

Produced by

DOWNTOWN
BOOKWORKS INC.

President   Julie Merberg
Senior Vice President   Patty Brown
Designer   Brian Michael Thomas/
                     Our Hero Productions

Special Thanks   Pam Abrams, Caroline Bronston,
                     Jackie Kristel, Emily Simon

10 11 12 13 14 TEP 10 9 8 7 6 5 4 3 2 1
ISBN-13: 978-0-7407-9962-4
ISBN-10: 0-7407-9962-2
Library of Congress Control Number: 2010922405

www.andrewsmcmeel.com

ATTENTION: SCHOOLS AND BUSINESSES

Andrews McMeel books are available at quantity discounts with bulk
purchase for educational, business, or sales promotional use. For
information, please write to: Special Sales Department, Andrews McMeel
Publishing, LLC, 1130 Walnut Street, Kansas City, Missouri 64106.

table of contents

leader of the pack

Taylor Lautner likes a challenge. When he found out that he might not be asked to reprise his role as sweet-guy-turned-hunky-werewolf Jacob Black in *New Moon*, he went straight to work. He hit the gym and packed on nearly 30 pounds of muscle to prove to the movie execs that fans would accept him in his newly expanded part. When the final casting choice came in, he was thrilled! And he was not alone. *Twilight* fans across the world—from both Team Edward and Team Jacob—had fought to keep Taylor in the series and were delighted that he'd be back. Not only would they get to see the same actor from one movie to the next, but they'd be seeing *a whole lot more* of him. Thanks to his wolfed-out character and some shirtless movie scenes, audiences would be able to check out close-ups of Taylor's hot bod in the second installment of the *Twilight* mega-series.

Read on to learn more about his early days as a martial artist, his years struggling to make it in Hollywood, and his big break in the 3-D hit *The Adventures of Sharkboy and Lavagirl*. Let us take you behind the scenes of *Twilight* and *New Moon* to see how Taylor delved into the role of Jacob Black, and find out what he has to say about fans, friends, and finding love.

The Real-Life Karate Kid

Tuesday, February 11, 1992, was a big day for the Lautner family. On that day, Deborah and Daniel Lautner welcomed their first child into the world. Taylor Daniel Lautner spent the first few years of his life in the suburbs of Grand Rapids, Michigan. His father was an airline pilot and his mother worked for an office furniture design company. Perhaps he was fated to one day portray a ferocious werewolf on the big screen—according to his parents, he was a biter in day care!

It is always a big help for a couple with a young child to have family in the same area, but the Lautners were especially lucky to have relatives nearby. One night, when Taylor was only four years old, he and his mother spent the night with an aunt. While they were away, the Lautner house caught

did you know?

Taylor was a great student! He told karateangels.com, "I get mostly As with an occasional A- here and there."

fire and burned to the ground. Taylor's father was traveling for work, so no one was at home when the devastating fire struck. Although they lost all of

their belongings, they were relieved and happy that no one was injured in the blaze. They moved into a bigger, nicer home that was even closer to some relatives in Hudsonville, Michigan. Two years later, there was a new addition to the Lautner trio.

Taylor's baby sister, Makena, was born.

At Jamestown Elementary School in Hudsonville, it became clear right away that Taylor was an athletic kid. He experimented with wrestling, baseball, and football (he's still a huge football fan!), before finding the perfect sport for himself. When he was only six years old, Taylor took his first karate class, and soon he was hooked!

At first, he was drawn to the silly

warm-up games, but as he began to take martial arts more seriously, his instructor took notice, too. When Taylor was seven, his teacher registered him for a karate competition in Louisville, Kentucky. No one could have known that his incredible performance there would set into motion a chain of events that would lead to superstardom.

popquiz

When Taylor first started taking martial arts lessons, one thing really bugged him. What was it?

Answer:
Working out barefoot. Taylor likes to keep his tootsies covered. And not much has changed—he still doesn't even like to wear sandals!

did you know?

In his very first competition,
Taylor took home three first-place
trophies. He also captured the interest
of an influential coach named Mike
Chat, an actor who had developed
his own supercharged, high-flying
blend of martial arts. He combined
elements from yoga, ballet, acrobatics,
kickboxing, tae kwon do, and other
physical disciplines to create XMA, or
"extreme martial arts."

Chat could tell right away that Taylor was a natural and invited him to attend Camp Chat International, his summer program in Los Angeles, California. As Taylor put it, he "fell in love" with XMA. "By the end of the camp, I was doing aerial cartwheels—with no hands!" Even though Mike was headquartered in California and Taylor lived in Michigan, the two kept in touch.

What is so special about XMA? As Taylor explained, "Regular martial arts is traditional, with no music and no flips choreographed into it." Extreme martial arts, on the other hand, features moves set to music. "It's very fast-beat, up-tempo and you put a lot of acrobatic maneuvers into the routine," he said. A true performer even at a young age, he was soon showing off his skills far and wide with Team Chat International. He even invented his own move called the corkscrew: "It's a backflip off one leg and then you do a 360 in the air and I land it in the splits." Taylor said. By

the time Taylor was eight years old, he had earned his black belt and beat out boys as old as 12 at the World Karate Federation Championships. At 11, he was ranked number one by the North American Sports Karate Association in his category. By 12, this real-life karate kid had won three Junior World Championships.

His commitment to performing, competing, and studying martial arts helped Taylor grow a lot. Not only did he learn discipline and dedication to a craft, he also perfected some awesome moves—moves that helped him land his first big movie role, tackle his own stunts in *New Moon*, and wow the audience as the host of *Saturday Night Live* in 2009.

"I love Taylor, he's my friend. . . . **Out of everybody in this movie, I think he's the one who stepped up in a way that's most impressive**. . . . He's growing into a really good guy, and he's really good in the movie. I'm so glad I can look at someone every day [while filming] and believe every word that they say."

—Kristen Stewart

21

Making Waves in Hollywood

With his amazing looks and outgoing personality, Taylor was destined for success outside of the karate circuit. His beloved coach, Mike Chat, encouraged Deb and Dan to take Taylor on some commercial auditions. Taylor laughed when he recalled his very first audition, which was for a Burger King ad: "I didn't even know what a pose was . . . but I

did you know?

Taylor can be seen in a tender lip-lock with lucky singer Cassi Thomson in the video for her song "Caught Up in You."

learned quickly and did some poses for them." Even though he did not land the part, this audition had a huge impact on him. The more he went on auditions, the more committed he was to becoming an actor. He had a lot going for him. He was charming and self-assured, athletic and focused, and had a bright, positive attitude that kept him from getting disillusioned when he didn't get the parts he wanted.

It is hard enough for a young actor to make it in the business, but there was one thing standing in the way of his next step. He still lived in Michigan. Hollywood was nearly 2,000 miles (3,200 km) away! Sometimes, Taylor and his folks would get a call at 9 or 10 p.m. about an audition the very next day. Taylor shared, "We'd leave really early in the morning and get there about noon. I'd go to the

audition in the afternoon, take the red-eye back to Grand Rapids, then go to school." He knew he couldn't continue with that crazy schedule. No matter how dedicated he was, a boy needs to get *some* sleep!

Together with his incredibly supportive family, Taylor had to make an agonizing decision: give up acting or pack up and relocate to Los Angeles. "Our family and friends did not want us to go," shared Taylor. "I told my parents I didn't want to give up acting. And after weighing the good with the bad, they agreed to move." Not wanting to make the decision too hastily, the Lautners moved to California for a month to try it out. There, Taylor trained

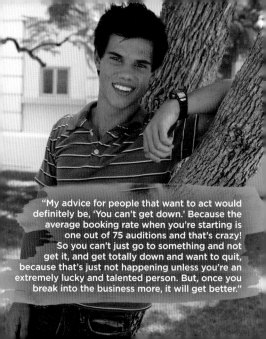

"My advice for people that want to act would definitely be, 'You can't get down.' Because the average booking rate when you're starting is one out of 75 auditions and that's crazy! So you can't just go to something and not get it, and get totally down and want to quit, because that's just not happening unless you're an extremely lucky and talented person. But, once you break into the business more, it will get better."

with his karate coach and paired up with an agent. Even though he heard the word "no" more times than he could count, he kept a positive outlook. "From karate, I had the confidence and drive to push myself," he said.

On what was supposed to be Taylor's last day in L.A., he got a

did you know?

Taylor had a small role on the TV show *Summerland*, which featured *High School Musical* heartthrob Zac Efron.

callback. It was just the little bit of encouragement he needed. The family extended its West Coast stay for another five months. He took time off from karate to dedicate his time to a constant parade of auditions, and eventually he earned a part in 2001's *Shadow Fury,* a movie about killer ninja clones. Next up, he scored a voiceover job for a *Rugrats Go Wild* ad campaign.

Taylor made his television debut with a small part on *The Bernie Mac*

Show. Later, he appeared on *The Nick and Jessica Variety Hour*, starring the then-husband-and-wife pair Nick Lachey and Jessica Simpson. In 2004, he played a bully in an episode of the sitcom starring Damon Wayans, *My Wife and Kids*. "That was fun because I'm normally not a bully because my parents wouldn't allow me to do that. I'm just not that person, but it was fun to experience something new." With every new role, no matter how small, Taylor learned more about the business. He also got to know many more casting directors and other movers and shakers on the scene in Los Angeles.

Taylor's big break came with the 2005 3-D hit *The Adventures of Sharkboy and Lavagirl*. His initial audition was just like any other. He met with the casting director and then went on his way. About two weeks later, Taylor got word that the director, Robert Rodriguez, and his son Racer wanted to meet with him. Racer was only seven years old at the time, but

did you know?

the plot of the movie had been all his idea. Here was a rare audition where impressing the director's son was superimportant! When Robert asked Taylor to pose like a superhero, he called on his years of XMA training and busted some serious moves. "I stood on one hand and I'm upside down and my legs are in a split position and his son really liked that." Unfortunately for Taylor, the search for the perfect

Sharkboy was only just beginning. The film team auditioned thousands of young actors, so it was a while before he got the news: He'd landed the biggest part of his career! When Taylor and his family learned he'd be Sharkboy, Taylor said they freaked out. "My whole family couldn't sleep for, like, a week."

Not only did his martial arts training help him win Racer's seal of approval, it also gave him

some extra responsibility on the set. Robert allowed him to choreograph one of his own fight scenes!

While working on *The Adventures of Sharkboy and Lavagirl*, Taylor pushed his imagination to the limit. Instead of telling the young actor all about his character, the director wanted Taylor to create his own vision of Sharkboy.

"Raised by sharks, he [Sharkboy] became very self-confident. And he winds up being half boy, half shark, occasionally going into these shark frenzies, where he starts biting and ripping stuff. He gets really, really crazy. And that's when you don't want to be near him. But he was fun to play because he got to do a lot of acrobatic stuff. And he gets to move like a shark and throw lots and lots of temper tantrums!"

And, because of the wacky, unrealistic setting of the movie, much of it was filmed in front of a green screen. That means that Taylor and the other actors were standing in front of a plain green backdrop during many of their scenes. While performing, they had to envision their surroundings and, in some cases, imagine the other characters that they were supposed to be acting with. "On the screen," Taylor explained, "you see like 'big ol' shark boat with turbo boosters,' and I'm just on this green box with two little handles."

first flashes of fame

Taylor had walked the red carpet a few times before the *Sharkboy and Lavagirl* premiere, but nothing could have prepared him for the insanity that was in store for him on June 4, 2005. "You wouldn't believe how many photographers are there!" he recalled. "'Taylor, turn over here. Turn to the right. Hold it here. To the left. Now over here.' It's really crazy on the red carpet, but knowing that it was your premiere made it even more fun."

Shortly after the film opened—and it was a hit!—he started to get recognized by fans. Unlike the throngs of screaming girls that he would encounter after *Twilight* opened, he was spotted first by guys close to his own age. "Ten-year-old boys were the ones who first recognized me. I'd be in a store, and boys would whisper to their moms. Then the moms would say, 'Excuse me—are you Sharkboy?'" Luckily, Taylor got

along well with his costars Taylor Dooley (who played Lavagirl) and Cayden Boyd (who played Max, the boy who dreamed up the superduo in the movie), so he had good company during that hectic time. Seemingly overnight, Taylor went from being a young aspiring actor trudging from audition to audition to having his own action figure!

The Boy Next Door

No matter how big a hit *The Adventures of Sharkboy and Lavagirl* was, nothing could possibly compare to the success of the *Twilight Saga*. When Taylor first auditioned for the film, he had no idea what he was getting into. Sure, his agent sounded a little more excited than usual about the movie, but Taylor hadn't even heard of the books (though

Twilight had spent 91 weeks on the *New York Times* best-seller list). When he got word that he was one of three guys on a short list for the part of Bella Swan's childhood friend and soon-to-be-werewolf love interest, he went online to get a little more information. Only then did he realize that *Twilight* was not going to be your average movie and that *Twilight* fans were something more than a handful of devoted book buffs. A month later, an ecstatic Taylor got the life-changing news: he'd won the coveted role of Jacob Black. Until then, he admitted, "I was not a vampire or werewolf fan at all."

As soon as he got the part, he sat down with the books to see what all

pop quiz

Who was the youngest of the *Twilight* stars: Taylor Lautner, Robert Pattinson, or Kristen Stewart?

Answer:
Taylor. He was only 16 years old on the set of *Twilight*. Kristen turned 18 while filming, and Robert was 21.

the hype was about and—not unlike the millions of others who have fallen under author Stephenie Meyer's spell—he got "hooked on them." In the series, Taylor felt readers could find a little bit of every genre. "There's romance, there's action-adventure, there's like a little horror in it, there's everything. So, I think that's why it attracts so many people, because it's a little mix of everything."

The character of Jacob isn't a huge part of the first installment of the story, but he is still very important. When Bella Swan's mother remarries, Bella returns to her childhood home of Forks, Washington, to live with her father. Jacob, an old friend with a puppy-dog

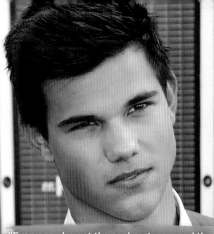

"Everyone else got the cool costumes and the makeup, the pale skin, and the colored contacts. All I got was this long black wig that reached halfway down my back. I hated it. It was the hottest, itchiest thing I've ever worn. I couldn't wait to get it off at the end of the day."

crush, welcomes her home, keeps an eye out for her, and warns her away from the mysterious Cullen family. Meanwhile, Bella is drawn to brooding, beautiful Edward Cullen (played by British heartbreaker Robert Pattinson), who turns out to be a 108-year-old vampire. Luckily for Bella, Edward and his family subsist on the blood of animals, not humans. An unexpected encounter with some violent, human-devouring vamps sets off a chain of events that puts Bella in mortal danger. It also kicks off an epic love triangle among good-guy vampire Edward, loyal and protective werewolf Jacob, and the lovely, down-to-earth Bella.

Taylor found the character incredibly interesting. "I love the way Stephenie wrote him," he revealed. "What I find cool is, like he has this Native American side who's just this happy-go-lucky kid, then he has this werewolf side where he's trying to hold back his temper and he wants to be violent." While striving to get his character right, he also tried hard not to be *too* nervous. Taking on a part that so many people cared so much about was stressful—he felt the pressure to please a lot of rabid fans. "But for the most part," he beamed, "I'm really just excited to be part of it."

taylor's type

Rolling Stone reporter Neil Strauss asked Taylor why he thought Jacob was so into Bella. And any girl who can proudly call herself a member of Team Jacob will want to know the answer: "Because she's different, meaning she's more of the plain-Jane type. You know, she's not fake." He confessed, "I know that attracts me, too. Just somebody who is down to earth and themselves."

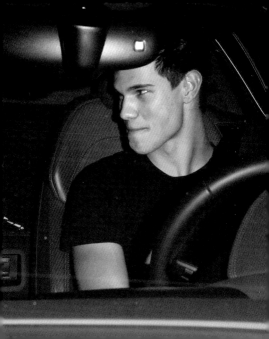

team jacob rocks

Twilight fans are a passionate bunch. They are split into two main camps: those who find Robert Pattinson and his character, Edward Cullen, to be the dreamiest onscreen boyfriend ever, and those who are rooting for Bella to end up with Jacob. As for Taylor, he could never quite understand Team Edward. As he put it, "Personally, I don't get the vampire thing. They're cold. Werewolves are hot. I mean, hot, cold, hot—come on!" He joked, "I think Bella is just confused at the moment. She doesn't know what's best for her and the Team Edward fans, but they'll come around. They'll come around."

Whether they are on Team Edward or Team Jacob, the fans have been the driving force behind the *Twilight* book series, and now they are there every step of the way through the movie saga, cheering on Taylor, Kristen, Robert, and all the rest of *Twilight*'s cool cast. Taylor is incredibly thankful for his

fans. He truly enjoys meeting them (though he admits that being asked to autograph a 40-something-year-old woman's Team Jacob undies was a little *too* crazy for him). And he's been known to stay out till 2 a.m. signing autographs, just so none of his fans go home empty-handed. Sometimes he feels overwhelmed by the throngs of screaming fans, but he knows that the movies wouldn't be successful without all of their energy and devotion.

Tackling New Moon

The character of Jacob Black grows up a lot from *Twilight* to *New Moon*. He transforms from the cute and clumsy boy next door into an intense, tall, broad-chested young man with a ferocious temper (and a hair-raising secret). Taylor wanted to make sure he'd be returning for the second movie, so he had to make a transformation,

did you know?

too. With the help of a personal trainer, a strict gym regimen, and a ridiculous number of calories, he managed to beef up and fill out, just like his character. To go from scrawny to brawny, he went to the gym five days a week for two hours a day. It took him a little while to find the right balance between working out a lot and working out *too* much and burning too many calories. And speaking of calories, his trainer had him on a strict food schedule (which is hard to call a diet!). "At one point," Taylor reported, "I had to shove as much food in my body as possible." To pack in the necessary 3,200 calories a

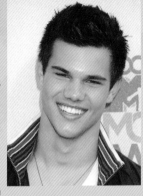

day, Taylor said, "I would literally have to carry a little baggy full of beef patties, raw almonds, sweet potatoes."

Getting bulked up enough to keep the part was only part of the battle.

Once Taylor knew he'd be playing
Jacob again, he had to get straight to
work on preparing for the new movie.
He certainly wasn't going to let the
Twihards down! In this part of the
story, Edward leaves Bella for her own
safety. She remains in Forks, bereft and
heartbroken. Jacob still harbors feelings
for his childhood pal and, as Taylor

joked, "Jacob has been waiting for this moment when he finds out that Edward has left Bella. He's like, 'Sweet—it's my turn!'" He helps to nurse Bella out of her depression. After he becomes a werewolf, he and his wolf pack try to protect his mortal love from the bloodthirsty vamps on her trail.

did you know?

Twilight was filmed in Oregon and *New Moon* was shot primarily in Vancouver, British Columbia. In most cases, similar buildings and locations were found and altered to match the first film, but the movie producers actually had to *build* a re-creation of Bella's house for *New Moon*.

Playing the new bulkier, moodier Jacob was a challenge for Taylor. Because he undergoes his transformation to becoming a werewolf in the middle of the film, he needed to be able to portray gentle, outgoing Jacob and fierce werewolf Jacob at any time during the filming. Taylor said, "It's like I'm playing a split personality, which is tricky, because sometimes I've had to play pre- and post-transformation Jacob on the same day of filming." It was also an amazing experience for him. "With *New Moon*," he explained, "it's not just the love story between these two anymore. Now there are three people, and it's dangerous."

native heritage

Taylor and his character, Jacob, are both friendly and outgoing, but they share more in common than that. Jacob is a member of the Quileute tribe, and Taylor comes from Native American ancestry. His mother is part Potawatomi and Ottawa Indian. Once known as a fierce tribe, the present-day Quileute are a group of about 750 people who mostly live in western Washington State.

Before filming *Twilight*, Taylor took some time to research his character. He read up on the Quileute tribe. He learned their myths and legends, and, before *New Moon*, he even spent some time with tribe members on the reservation. Taylor reported, "I'd have to say that the biggest surprise for me was learning that the kids are just like me." They enjoyed playing baseball and football—just like Taylor. "Somehow we got on the topic of what they like to do for fun, and they go to the beach and check out girls."

Another thing that impressed Taylor about the young Quileute men he met was their sense of community. He noticed that they didn't need to be reminded to do things like taking out the trash. They were constantly helping one another. Taylor took that to heart. He really wanted to bring that sense of mindfulness to his portrayal of Jacob.

On Set with Taylor

Before a typical day on the *New Moon* set, Taylor would be up and out of bed by 4:30 or 5 a.m. Then he'd work until 5 or 6 p.m. After that, he enjoyed relaxing with his costars and exploring the restaurants in town. The filming process could get pretty intense. Whether he was battling the elements or doing his own stunts, Taylor worked hard!

One of his favorite scenes was the breakup scene. It's the first time Bella has seen Jacob since his transformation. The scene packed an emotional punch, but it wasn't filmed in the most pleasant conditions. "It was also painful to shoot because it was 35 degrees and we had rain poured on us. It was 'rain tower' rain, which is straight from the spring and it was freezing." He went on to say, "It was bad, and I wasn't really wearing much." (Which doesn't sound all that bad to his fans!)

He also really liked some of his more physical scenes—such as the dirt bike sequences. He'd never ridden a dirt bike before, and even though it's only for a few seconds in the movie, he

had to practice a lot. According to humble Taylor, the big problem wasn't *riding* the bike, but *looking good* while he did it. "I got to hop on the bike and go really fast and come to a skidding halt. It's really cool," he reported.

Taylor also got to do some of his own wirework. When he runs up the side of Bella's house, he is hooked up to wires to keep him safe. "The wires were there so if I slipped and fell I didn't face-plant into the ground. But it was definitely challenging," he said. "You need to be on. I'm using a little plug in the side of the wall to take off from and jump, so it's really complicated and it required a lot of practice." In fact, it was the last bit that he filmed and he said he practiced that stunt for three hours a day every weekend.

Another memorable moment came when he filmed the scene where Jacob

pop quiz

Taylor has a Maltese dog.
What is her name?

Answer:
Roxy.

transforms midair. Stunt coordinators used cables and harnesses to help Taylor freeze in midair, but it was challenging to get it just right. All of the people who worked on that scene were impressed by how much control he had over his body. Stunt coordinator J. J. Makaro declared him a "natural," and said Taylor had the makings of a great stuntman.

Of all of the books in the *Twilight* series, Taylor has declared *Eclipse* as his top pick, largely because the Edward-Bella-Jacob love triangle is at its height. There is a scene in *Eclipse* that ranks as one of his all-time faves. "The tent scene, where Edward is forced, and I guess it was a choice of his, to let me

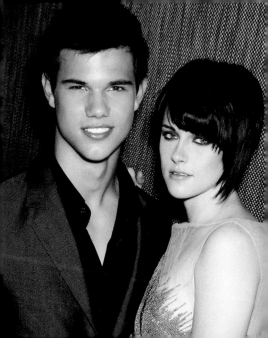

sleep in the same sleeping bag as Bella just so she doesn't die, because she's shivering to death and I'm warm. I'm the only thing at that moment that can keep her alive. There's a lot of ribbing going on between Jacob and Edward. It's going to be a really good movie and visually stunning."

Another standout moment for Taylor on the *Eclipse* set involves Jacob's Native American culture. He actually gets to speak a little of the Quileute language. As he leans in to kiss Bella, he says something in the ancient language. "And no, I'm not gonna tell you what I said. I'll leave that to you to figure out," he said. "But it was really cool. There's only like four people left

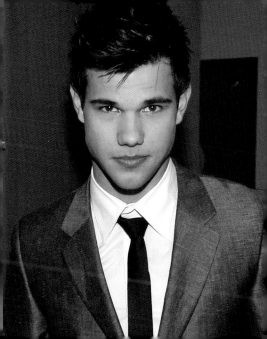

in the world that actually speak Quileute so we were able to talk to one of these ladies."

From "*Twilight* moms" and new workout routines to bonding with costars, performing his own wire stunts, and speaking a rare language, Taylor experienced a lot in a short time. With the rest of the *Twilight Saga* still in production, he is certain to go through so much more. And Taylor fans are sure to follow along every step of the way.

did you know?

Taylor's astrological sign is Aquarius.

more movie magic

In the short break between working on *New Moon* and *Eclipse*, Taylor found the time to film *Valentine's Day*, which featured an incredible roster of A-listers including hotties such as Ashton Kutcher, Topher Grace, Jamie Foxx, and Patrick Dempsey. Taylor shared his screen time with one special lady: pop princess Taylor Swift. Starring as the prom king and queen, the duo engaged in some sexy lip-locks that drove Team Jacob fans wild. After *Valentine's Day* and *Eclipse*, he is set to appear in *Northern Lights*, a movie about four young pilots who compete in flying competitions. Then it is back to the *Twilight* camp for *Breaking Dawn*.

Beyond that, who knows what is in store for Taylor Lautner? He put himself and his body through a pretty serious transformation for the role of Jacob Black in the *Twilight Saga*. When asked if he would do something like that again, he replied, "A year from now,

if I love a story and I love a character that requires me to lose 40 pounds, I'm ready to do it." From sweet boy next door and hot-blooded werewolf to prom queen–smooching track star or high-flying action star, he's proven that he's got what it takes to keep audiences coming back for more.

taylor dishes on his colleagues

About Actor George Lopez:
"George Lopez was great, too. We had paper wad fights while we were shooting. . . . He was a lot of fun, too!"

About Actress Kristen Stewart:
"Kristen's awesome! She's an amazing actress and she's an awesome girl. She's a lot of fun."

About Actor Bronson Pelletier:
"Jared [character in *New Moon*] is a funny guy, a real jokester—and Bronson, who plays him, in real life is the same way, so he does that well."

About Actress Bryce Dallas Howard:
"Bryce is amazing. She's extremely talented and a great girl as well."

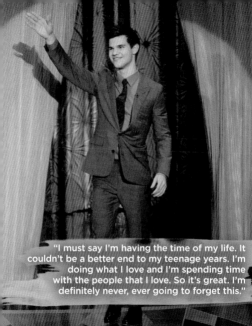

"I must say I'm having the time of my life. It couldn't be a better end to my teenage years. I'm doing what I love and I'm spending time with the people that I love. So it's great. I'm definitely never, ever going to forget this."

PHOTO CREDITS